Table of Contents

Throughout the book provision is made for making estimations and calculations in the U.S. customary system or in the metric system or both.

Trends in Mathematics Education and Testing

Years ago, mathematics in school consisted mostly of pencil-and-paper calculations. More recently, emphasis has shifted to problem solving based on real-life situations. Rather than manipulating numbers that don't represent anything, students are asked to work with real materials and real situations involving time, measurement, and money.

Testing in the schools has been changing recently too. Instead of "filling in the bubble" on multiple choice answer sheets, students are asked to show their reasoning and their calculations. They are asked to represent the problems and the solutions with written narratives and graphics.

Calculators are being used more often than before, especially with problems involving very large numbers. Teachers often emphasize the use of estimation to check how reasonable a calculator answer is. Just as current trends are intended to correct a possible overemphasis on pencil calculations, these trends should also guard against going too far to the opposite extreme by excluding pencil math. It is important that mathematical instruction and activities are balanced. Effective programs provide a mixture of mental math, paper-and-pencil math, and calculator math.

Dear Parents,

In your child's class, we are trying to show the many ways that math is used in the real world. One of the ways you can be helpful would be to involve your child in the planning of any vacations or other trips you might be considering.

Draw your child's attention to the way your travel planning involves estimations and calculations with distance, time, and money. In our class, we will do several activities involving these mathematical concepts and skills, focusing on imaginary places. Then, as a follow-up, I will provide your child with activity sheets to be used in applying what was learned to real or imaginary trips to real places.

When you include your child in the planning of your actual family trips, he or she will be ready to participate and to get the maximum value from your discussions and travels.

Your Child's Teacher,

Where Shall We Go?
Teacher Instructions

The sections in this book start with a classroom activity focusing on an imaginary situation. This is followed by one or more application activities dealing with real situations.

Students add the distances for various "legs" of an imaginary journey that has several stops in the introductory activity of this unit. Calculations are done with both miles and kilometers, but do not involve converting units of distance within or between the two systems. Younger students can just round off the distances before adding them up. Older students may be able to add the distances including fractions of miles and tenths of kilometers.

On page 5, students are asked to calculate travel distances for a variety of imaginary vacation trips.

Page 6 applies the same skills to actual trips that the students would like to take. These trips are in three categories; 1-day trips, 3-day trips, and 1-week trips. To prepare for this activity, round up some roadmaps and atlases and show your students how they can determine distances from these maps in two ways:

- Distances shown on major roads between cities

- Scale ratios and references

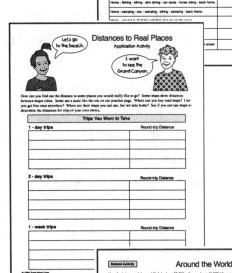

Page 7 is an activity that offers a race around the world involving a variety of vehicles. This is a good activity for showing students how to first make estimates, then check their accuracy using calculators.

How Far is It?
Introductory Activity

Here is a map of *Vacationland*. The distances between the various vacation spots are shown in two ways: miles and kilometers. Add up the total distance for each trip described in the chart at the bottom of this page.

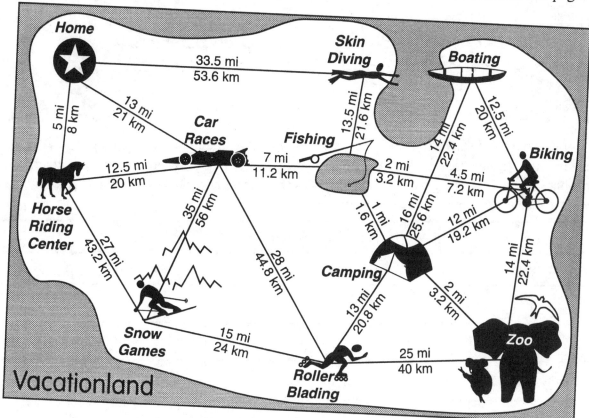

Round Trip	Distance	
	miles	kilometers
Home - horse riding - snow games - roller blading - car races - back home.		
Home - skin diving - fishing - car races - back home.		
Home - car races - fishing - skin diving - camping - roller blading - snow games - horse riding - back home.		
Home - boating - zoo - camping - car races - back home.		
Home - fishing - biking - skin diving - car races - horse riding - back home.		
Home - camping - zoo - camping - biking - camping - back home.		
Home - around to all of the activities that are on the coast until reaching home again.		
Home - shortest route to do all the activities that are *not* on the coast and back to home.		
Home - shortest route to do all the activities involving water (except snow) and back home.		

Math on a Trip

Distances to Real Places

Application Activity

Let's go to the beach.

I want to see the Grand Canyon.

How can you find out the distance to some places you would really like to go? Some maps show distances between major cities. Some use a scale like the one on our practice page. Where can you buy road maps? Can you get free ones anywhere? Where are there maps you can use, but not take home? See if you can use maps to determine the distances for trips of your own choice.

Trips You Want to Take

1 - day trips

	Round-trip Distance

2 - day trips

	Round-trip Distance

1 - week trips

	Round-trip Distance

Around the World

How far is it around the world? It is about 25,000 miles or about 40,000 kilometers. If you could actually make an around-the-world trip with each of the vehicles below, how long would it take? You can find out by dividing the distance of the trip by the distance the vehicle travels in one hour. That will tell you how many hours the total trip will take.

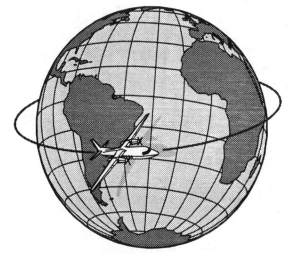

If it takes more than 24 hours, divide the hours by 24 to get days.

If it takes more than 7 days, divide by 7 to get weeks.

If it takes more than 4 weeks, divide by 4 to get months.

This is a good project for a calculator.

Vehicles	Approximate Speeds		Time to Make the Trip
walking	5 mi/hr	8 km/hr	_____
bike	30 mi/hr	48 km/hr	_____
car	65 mi/hr	100 km/hr	_____
train	100 mi/hr	160 km/hr	_____
prop plane	250 mi/hr	400 km/hr	_____
jet plane	500 mi/hr	800 km/hr	_____
orbiting capsule	17,500 mi/hr	28,000 km/hr	_____

What Shall We Do?
Teacher Instructions

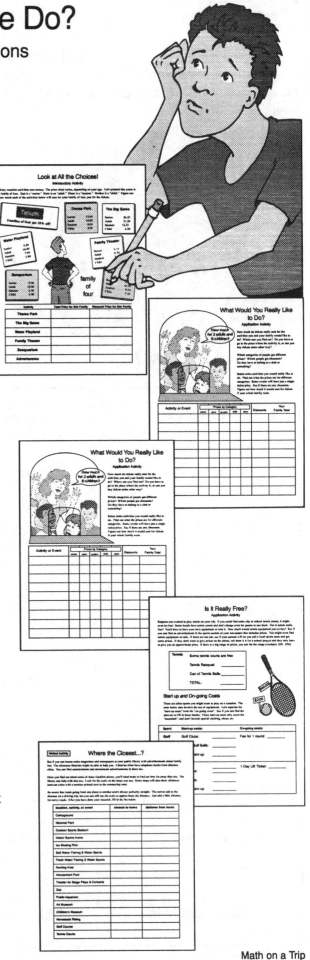

The activities on pages 9-13 start with the costs of a vacation activity beyond just the price of admission. To make the mathematics interesting, different family members pay different rates, and there is a family discount.

Page 9 deals with imaginary activities.

Page 10 asks the students to apply what they learned to real activities that they would actually like to do. It deals with an imaginary family of four.

Page 11 has the students do their math based on their own family. Some of your students may not have either a mother or father at home. They may be living with relatives or perhaps adults that are not relatives. Students can define "family" as they wish for this activity. This activity brings in the expenses that youngsters may not think about when considering the cost of an activity. Students can select whichever type of activity they wish for this cost analysis, and then compare their results with other students.

The activity on page 12 highlights the difference between start-up (equipment) costs for participating in a sport versus the ongoing costs that come up each time you play.

On page 13, students will determine the distances to the closest place where a variety of family activities can be found. This activity involves the use of advertisements, telephone books, roadmaps, and atlases. Students are encouraged to find out which of these kinds of materials are available at the public library.

Math on a Trip

Look at All the Choices!

Introductory Activity

Many vacation activities cost money. The price often varies, depending on your age. Let's pretend that yours is a family of four. Dad is a "senior." Mom is an "adult." Sister is a "student." Brother is a "child." Figure out how much each of the activities below will cost for your family of four, just for the tickets.

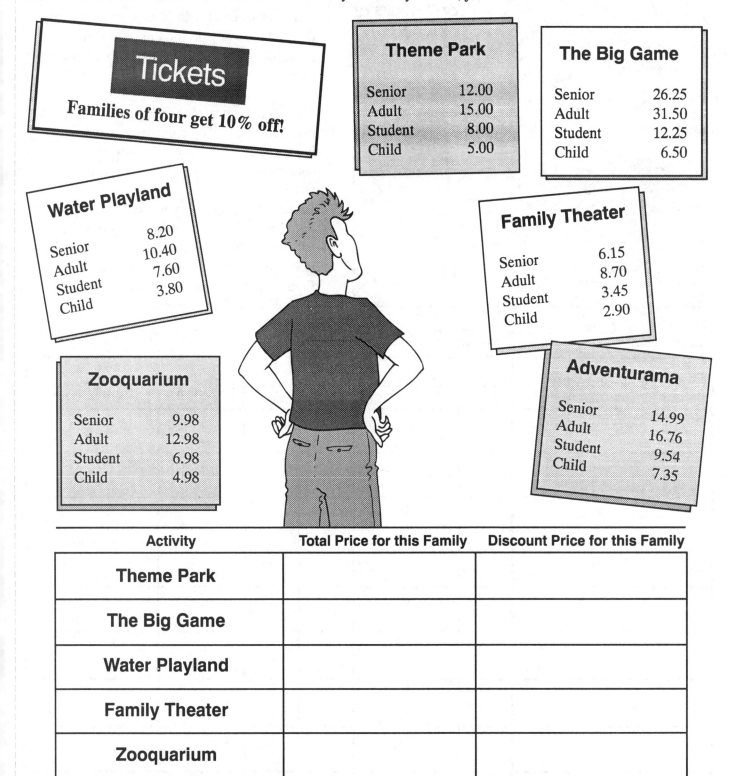

Tickets

Families of four get 10% off!

Theme Park

Senior	12.00
Adult	15.00
Student	8.00
Child	5.00

The Big Game

Senior	26.25
Adult	31.50
Student	12.25
Child	6.50

Water Playland

Senior	8.20
Adult	10.40
Student	7.60
Child	3.80

Family Theater

Senior	6.15
Adult	8.70
Student	3.45
Child	2.90

Zooquarium

Senior	9.98
Adult	12.98
Student	6.98
Child	4.98

Adventurama

Senior	14.99
Adult	16.76
Student	9.54
Child	7.35

Activity	Total Price for this Family	Discount Price for this Family
Theme Park		
The Big Game		
Water Playland		
Family Theater		
Zooquarium		
Adventurama		

What Would You Really Like to Do?

Application Activity

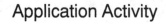

How much for 2 adults and 10 children?

How much do tickets really cost for the activities you and your family would like to do? Where can you find out? Do you have to go to the place where the activity is, or can you buy tickets some other way?

Which categories of people get different prices? Which people get discounts? Do they have to belong to a club or something?

Select some activities you would really like to do. Find out what the prices are for different categories. Some events will have just a single ticket price. See if there are any discounts. Figure out how much it would cost for tickets if your whole family went.

Activity or Event	Prices by Category					Discounts	Your Family Total
	senior	adult	student	child	other		

Family Activities Have Hidden Costs

Application Activity

There's more to going to a game than just buying the tickets. Have your parents tell you approximately how much the things in the list below cost. Then see how much it would cost for the four-member family described on the right to go to the game.

> There are two parents. Two of the children go to the game, but the baby stays home with a sitter.
>
> Assume that each family member will get a sandwich and drink.
>
> At another time, each family member will get a snack (popcorn, peanuts, ice cream, etc.).
>
> The two children at the game will each get a souvenir.
>
> There will be a fee for parking at the sports center.
>
> The babysitter will charge an hourly fee.

Ask your parents what the approximate prices would be for all of these things. They may also think of some other expenses that aren't listed here. Using the prices your parents supply, figure out the total cost for this family to go to the game:

1 adult ticket = _____ x 2 = _____

1 child ticket = _____ x 2 = _____

1 sandwich = _____ x 4 = _____

1 soft drink = _____ x 4 = _____

1 snack = _____ x 4 = _____

1 souvenir = _____ x 2 = _____

car parking = _____ x 1 = _____

babysitter for 1 hour = _____ x 5 hrs = _____

other costs (describe) = _____ _____

TOTAL: [   ]

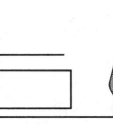

Is it Really Free?
Application Activity

Suppose you wanted to play tennis on your trip. If you could find some city or school tennis courts, it might even be free! Some hotels have tennis courts and don't charge extra for guests to use them. But is tennis really free? You'd have to have your own equipment or rent it. How much would tennis equipment cost to buy? See if you can find an advertisement in the sports section of your newspaper that includes prices. You might even find tennis equipment on sale. If there are not ads, see if your parents will let you call a local sports store and get some prices. If they don't want to give prices on the phone, tell them it is for a school project and they only have to give you an approximate price. If there is a big range in prices, you can list the range (example: $30 - $50).

Tennis	Some tennis courts are free
	Tennis Racquet: _____
	Can of Tennis Balls: _____
	TOTAL: _____

Start up *and* Ongoing Costs

There are other sports you might want to play on a vacation. The ones below also involve the use of equipment. Let's separate the "start-up costs" from the "ongoing costs." See if you can find the answers to fill in these blanks. These start-up costs only cover the "essentials," and don't include special clothing, shoes, etc.

Sport:	Start-up costs:		Ongoing costs:
Golf	Golf clubs:	_____	Fee for 1 round: _____
	Box of golf balls:	_____	
	Basic start-up:	_____	
Skiing	Skis:	_____	1-day lift ticket: _____
	Ski poles:	_____	
	Ski boots:	_____	
	Basic start-up:	_____	

Where is the Closest...?

See if you can locate some magazines and newspapers at your public library with advertisements about family fun. The reference librarian might be able to help you. Libraries often have telephone books from distant cities. You can find entertainment and amusement advertisements in there too.

Once you find out about some of these vacation places, you'll need maps to find out how far away they are. The library can help with that too. Look for the scale on the maps you use. Some maps will also show distances between cities with a number printed next to the connecting road.

Be aware that roads going from one place to another aren't always perfectly straight. The curves add to the distance on a driving trip, but you can still use the scale to approximate the distance. Just add a little distance for curvy roads. After you have done your research, fill in the list below:

Location, activity, or event	Closest to home	Distance from home
Campground		
National Park		
Outdoor Sports Stadium		
Indoor Sports Arena		
Ice Skating Rink		
Salt Water Fishing & Water Sports		
Fresh Water Fishing & Water Sports		
Hunting Area		
Amusement Park		
Theater for Stage Plays & Concerts		
Zoo		
Public Aquarium		
Art Museum		
Children's Museum		
Horseback Riding		
Golf Course		
Tennis Courts		

How Will We Get There?
Teacher Instructions

Brainstorm with your students about the variety of ways to get where they would like to go. Show them that there are several factors involved in choosing. Here is a sample of how the discussion might go as you compare and contrast the choices with your class:

How about going by plane?
Say, that sounds great. We'd get there really fast. But... wait a minute. It's pretty expensive. And, how would we get around after we got there without a car to use?

How about going by train?
Wouldn't that be fun? But...it would take longer than a plane. We wouldn't have as much time at the place we're going. How about the meals? I hear they're expensive on a train.

How about going by bus?
Yeah...a bus is less expensive than a train, isn't it? And they don't have those expensive meals. Wait a minute...they don't have meals at all? Where will we eat? And we still won't have a car to use at the other end, unless we rent one.

How about going by boat?
How could we go by boat, unless the places we are going are next to water? But cruising is terrific. You can unpack and your hotel room goes with you. They have terrific food and everything is paid for in advance...no surprises.

How about going by car?
Now we're getting more practical! It's not as expensive as those other ways. But hold on! It will take so long to get there. We'll spend half of our vacation time in the car. That wouldn't be so bad if there were some interesting things to see along the way.

How about going by camper?
Wow...the best of both worlds! We'll save all those motel costs and we can cook our own meals. But...who's got a camper? We don't have one. Can you rent a camper? How much does it cost? How about the insurance?

After this opening discussion, use pages 15-19 to get your students involved with the mathematics of making transportation choices. The activity on page 16 involves interviewing of travel agents. If your school is in an area with only one or a few travel agents, you may want to run the activity with groups rather than individuals, and send only a group representative to interview the agent. Another approach would be to bring the travel agent to class as a guest speaker.

Comparing Choices of Transportation
Introductory Activity

Let's compare the costs for a ten-day vacation for one person, with each of three people getting there using a different kind of transportation. Let's make a comparison. This is oversimplified, but it will help to make a point about judging costs just on ticket price.

Let's assume that each day a person spends at the vacation hotel will cost $70 for lodging plus three meals averaging $10 each. This means each day at the hotel costs:

$70
+$30
⎯⎯⎯
☐

Traveler 1

takes a **plane** costing $400 round trip. That is $ _____ each way. Meals are provided at no extra charge on the plane. Here's how the basic expenses look on a day-to-day basis:

DAY	1	2	3	4	5	6	7	8	9	10	TOTAL
	plane	hotel	hotel	hotel	hotel	hotel	hotel	hotel	hotel	**plane**	
	$200	$100	$100	$100	$100	$100	$100	$100	$100	$200	

plane

Traveler 2

takes a **train** because the ticket costs less than the plane, only $380 round trip. Meals aren't provided free on the train. They are $20 each. That means you spend $60 per day on the train for food, and you are on the train for two days each way. If you divide the ticket price by four and add the $60 for food, you get the price per day for taking the train:

DAY	1	2	3	4	5	6	7	8	9	10	TOTAL
	train	**train**	hotel	hotel	hotel	hotel	hotel	hotel	**train**	**train**	
	$155	$155	$100	$100	$100	$100	$100	$100	$155	$155	

train

Traveler 3

takes the **bus** because the ticket costs less than either the plane or the train, $340 round trip. The bus is slower, so you're on the road three days each way. There are no meals on the bus and you stop each night to stay at an inexpensive motel. Meals near the motels average $10 and the motels average $50 per night. Each day on the road by bus is $30 for meals, $50 for a motel, and 1/6 of $360 for the bus. That adds up to a daily road cost of:

DAY	1	2	3	4	5	6	7	8	9	10	TOTAL
	bus	**bus**	**bus**	hotel	hotel	hotel	hotel	**bus**	**bus**	**bus**	
	$140	$140	$140	$100	$100	$100	$100	$140	$140	$140	

bus

In this example:

Which turns out to be the most expensive choice of transportation? _____

Which turns out to be the least expensive choice of transportaion? _____

With which choice does the traveler get the least time at the hotel? _____

Comparing Airline Rates and Services
Application Activity

You can do some comparison shopping about transportation. Interview a travel agent by phone or in person or call some airlines on their toll-free numbers. Check with your parents before using either approach. If there is only one travel agent in your area, you may want to have one class member do the interviewing for your group or class, perhaps involving more than one destination.

Select a major population area that your family would really like to visit that is far from where you live. Have the agent review the airline options. Prices vary from one time to the next, so ask about the *range* of prices for each option. When are prices high and when are they low? Are there different prices for different passengers flying on the same airline or even on the same plane? What is included in the fare? Snacks? Meals? Special diets? Movies? Wheelchairs? Are there any "no-frills" airlines?

Fill in the chart below. Compare your information with what other students find out.

Destination:				
Airline	Highest Regular Fare	Lowest Regular Fare	Special Fares	Services Included

Are You a Frequent Flier?

If you fly often enough, some airlines will give you special prizes. Look at these:

SkyFly Airlines				
If you fly this far:			**You will get:**	
25,000 mi	or	40,000 km	*Prize 1*	seat in first class
30,000 mi	or	48,000 km	*Prize 2*	1-day rental car
35,000 mi	or	56,000 km	*Prize 3*	free trip in country
40,000 mi	or	64,000 km	*Prize 4*	free trip anywhere

Use a piece of string to measure the approximate distances for the trips below on a world globe. There will be a scale on the globe to tell you how much an inch or a centimeter of string is worth in miles or kilometers.

Write in the distances and the prizes each traveler would earn from SkyFly Airlines on the chart below.

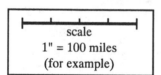

scale
1" = 100 miles
(for example)

Trip	Distance Traveled	Prize
Fifteen round trips between Los Angeles and Washington, D.C.		
A triangular round trip of Anchorage to Tierra del Fuego to Helsinki and back to Anchorage		
A trip from Montreal to Rio de Janeiro to London to Tokyo to Melbourne to Honolulu to Los Angeles		
A trip completely around the world following the equator		
Two round trips from San Francisco to New Delhi and back (Be sure to go the shortest way, over the North Pole.)		

Math on a Trip

Let's Rent a Car

Every car rental company claims to be the best. It's hard to tell which offers the best deal because there are so many factors involved. See which offer below is the best, based on this trip, based only on the cost. Of course, there are other factors involved in making a choice.

You want a car for three days in a U.S. city: Friday, Saturday, and Sunday. You plan to drive the car less than 600 miles.

RATTLING RENTS
$ 30 per weekday
$ 15 per weekend day
$ 10 per 100 miles or portion thereof

Comfy Cars
$ 45 per day
No charge for mileage

Awesome Autos
$ 50 per weekday
$ 25 per weekend day
$ 5 per 100 miles or portion thereof

VROOOM RENTALS
$ 25 per weekday
$ 20 per weekend day
$ 10 per 100 miles or portion thereof

List the rental companies below in order from the best deal to the worst with the total cost for each:

Company	Total Cost
1.	
2.	
3.	
4.	

Let's Take the Bus

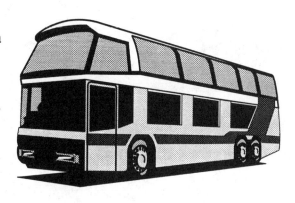

That's the trouble. If you fly to the vacation spot, you won't have a car when you get there. If you can't afford a rental car, you'll have to use public transportation.

Bus drivers usually want you to have exact change when you climb on the bus. Write down the bills and coins you would need to pay the bus fares for each ride your family takes below. The first one shows you how to write it. In each case, use the smallest number of coins and bills that you can, listing them in order from the highest values down to the lowest.

Fare $2.36	**Fare $1.72**	**Fare $0.91**	**Fare $1.33**
_1_ . _____	_____ . _____	_____ . _____	_____ . _____
_1_ . _____	_____ . _____	_____ . _____	_____ . _____
_____ . _25_	_____ . _____	_____ . _____	_____ . _____
_____ . _10_	_____ . _____	_____ . _____	_____ . _____
_____ . _1_	_____ . _____	_____ . _____	_____ . _____
_____ . _____	_____ . _____	_____ . _____	_____ . _____

Fare $1.91	**Fare $0.43**	**Fare $3.36**	**Fare $0.67**
_____ . _____	_____ . _____	_____ . _____	_____ . _____
_____ . _____	_____ . _____	_____ . _____	_____ . _____
_____ . _____	_____ . _____	_____ . _____	_____ . _____
_____ . _____	_____ . _____	_____ . _____	_____ . _____
_____ . _____	_____ . _____	_____ . _____	_____ . _____
_____ . _____	_____ . _____	_____ . _____	_____ . _____

Math on a Trip

Where Will We Stay?
Teacher Instructions

A good way to start these activities is to ask your students how much they think the rates are for:

- a fancy hotel
- a nice hotel
- a cheap hotel
- a motel
- a bed and breakfast
- a campground

When your students guess at the rates, you will most likely find that the range of answers will vary widely. After you have brainstormed this issue, provide your students with some resource materials to see what the realities are. Auto club books, motel catalogs, travel brochures, travel magazines, and advertisements are usually easy to get at little or no cost.

After your students have gotten the "feel" for these resources and how to use them, use page 21 as a classroom activity. Then, page 22 could be used either as a classroom or a take-home activity.

You might want to invite an auto club employee to come into your classroom as a guest speaker and to answer students' questions about travel and travel costs.

 Math on a Trip

What Is the "Bottom Line"?

Introductory Activity

Compare these prices to see which would be least expensive for a family with 2 adults and 2 children.

Motels listed in order of least to most expensive.	Total Price for this Family

Comparing Lodging Choices
Application Activity

Try a little comparison shopping for lodging
at a place your family would really like to go to.

1. Pick a location with lots of motels.

2. Find books with motel listings.

Possible sources:

- Automobile Clubs

- Local Chain Motels

- Travel Agencies

- Public Library

3. Pick five motels to compare.

4. Write down each motel's prices for the four options on the chart below.

5. See if they offer any discounts for Auto Club or other memberships, or for Frequent Fliers, etc. You may have to call their toll-free number to get this information. Ask your parents first.

6. Based on the information you have gathered, figure out what your family would be charged at each motel, including any discounts for which your family qualifies.

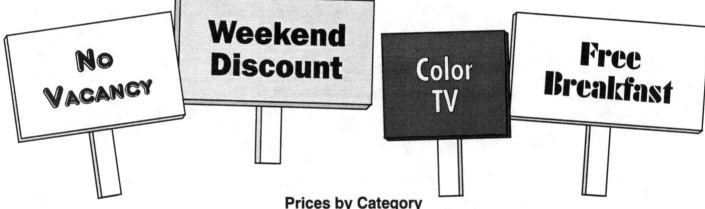

Prices by Category

Motel	1 person	2 people 1 bed	2 people 2 beds	extra person	Discounts	*Your* Family Total

How About a Trailer?

Should we rent or buy?

A trailer looks pretty tempting. With a trailer, you avoid the cost of staying in motels when you are on the road. You still have to pay for a place to park your trailer, but that costs less than a motel. With a trailer, you can cook your own meals. That saves money too.

One of the choices would be to *rent* a trailer.

If a trailer rents for $50 per day, how much would it cost your family for a two-week (14- day) vacation?

Another choice would be to *buy* a trailer.

If the trailer costs $15,000 new, your family would probably have to borrow the money. Suppose the interest on the loan totaled $4,200 if you paid the loan off in four years. How much would the trailer cost altogether?

How many months are there in one year?

How many months are there in four years?

What would your monthly payments be if you were to pay off the total cost for the new trailer over the four-year period?

How does that monthly payment compare to what it costs to rent the trailer?

The only way that buying the trailer would be a good idea for financial reasons would be if you used the trailer a lot more than just 14 days per year. How many rental days per year would cost the same as buying the trailer with the loan described above?

About how many months is that?

This little exercise helps to show how you can compare renting to buying, but the prices may not be accurate for your area or for the type of trailer you would like. See if you can find out the actual prices for trailer rentals and purchases in your area. Also check on how much interest you would have to pay on a loan of the size you would need. Then follow the procedure here to make a real comparison.

 Math on a Trip

How Long Will It Take?
Teacher Instructions

Review with your students the ways that maps show distances: written on segments of main roads between cities, and shown as scale references.

Once the distance to a travel site is known, your students can determine about how long it will take to get there if they use an average driving speed. 50 miles per hour (80 km/hr) is often used as a convenient average, assuming that most of the trip will be on the open road.

Show your students that they can determine the approximate driving time by using this formula:

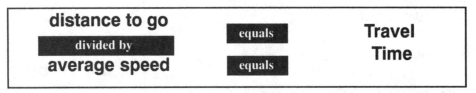

The same formula can also be applied to longer trips taken on a plane. Instead of an average driving speed of 50 mph, you can use an average flying time of 500 mi/hr (800 km/hr). Maps of the world won't have distances shown between individual cities like local maps do, but they do have scale references.

Travel time comes out the same whether miles are divided by mi/hr, or kilometers are divided by km/hr. Here is an example:

$$\frac{250 \text{ mi}}{50 \text{ mi/hr}} = 5 \text{ hours}$$
travel time

$$\frac{400 \text{ km}}{80 \text{ km/hr}} = 5 \text{ hours}$$
travel time

On page 25, your students will estimate driving times, using the map right on the page. On page 26, students will estimate travel times for both driving and flying trips to actual locations.

Remind your students that these will be approximations, but that approximations can be very helpful in planning a trip. Good travel planning also includes backup plans just in case things don't go the way you expect.

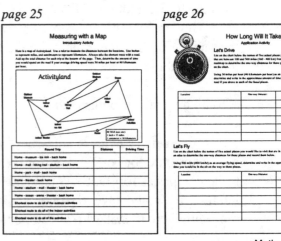

page 25   *page 26*

Math on a Trip

Measuring with a Map
Introductory Activity

Here is a map of *Activityland*. Use a ruler to measure the distances between the locations. Use inches to represent miles, and centimeters to represent kilometers. Always take the shortest route with a road. Add up the total distance for each trip at the bottom of the page. Then, determine the amount of time you would spend on the road if your average driving speed were 50 miles per hour or 80 kilometers per hour.

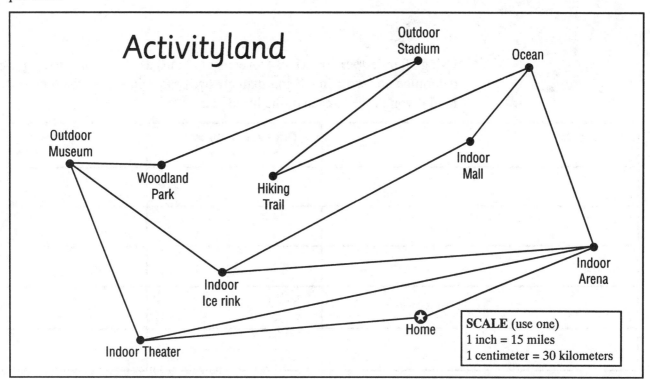

Activityland

Outdoor Stadium
Ocean
Outdoor Museum
Woodland Park
Hiking Trail
Indoor Mall
Indoor Ice rink
Indoor Arena
Home
Indoor Theater

SCALE (use one)
1 inch = 15 miles
1 centimeter = 30 kilometers

Round Trip	Distance	Driving Time
Home - museum - ice rink - back home		
Home - mall - hiking trail - stadium - back home		
Home - park - mall - back home		
Home - theater - back home		
Home - stadium - mall - theater - back home		
Home - ocean - arena - theater - back home		
Shortest route to do all of the outdoor activities		
Shortest route to do all of the indoor activities		
Shortest route to do all of the activities		

How Long Will It Take?

Application Activity

Let's Drive

List on the chart below the names of five actual places you would like to visit that are between 100 and 500 miles (160 - 800 km) from your home. Use a roadmap to determine the one-way distances for these places, and record them on the chart.

Using 50 miles per hour (80 kilometers per hour) as an average driving speed, determine and write in the approximate amount of time you would be on the road if you drove to each of the listed places.

Location:	One-way Distance:	Driving Time:

Let's Fly

List on the chart below the names of five actual places you would like to visit that are in distant countries. Use an atlas to determine the one-way distances for these places and record them below.

Using 500 mi/hr (800 km/hr) as an average flying speed, determine and write in the approximate amounts of time you would be in the air on the way to these places.

Location:	One-way Distance:	Flying Time:

Math on a Trip

Lost your Luggage?

How terrible! Your parents' suitcase fell off the back of your rental car. The tour bus behind you knocked it over the side into a river full of alligators! But don't worry. Your parents have insurance that will cover part of it.

Fill out the claim form below and find out how much the insurance company will pay. The amount paid for the loss of one of each type of item is shown.

Insurance Form			
	number lost	allowance for one	Total allowance per category
shirts	7	12.00	
blouses	5	14.00	
sweaters	3	13.00	
coats	4	25.00	
pants	6	18.00	
skirts	5	15.00	
dresses	4	20.00	
underwear	15	5.00	
shoes (pairs)	4	20.00	
stockings (pairs)	16	3.00	
belts	2	9.00	
ties	3	6.00	
		Subtotal	
The company does not pay for the first $200 of the loss. This is referred to as a "deductible."		**Deductible**	- 2 0 0 . 0 0
		Grand Total	

When Will We Get There?
Teacher Instructions

The driver can get pretty irritated when these questions are coming up every ten minutes.

You can teach your students how to figure out the answer to these questions for themselves. Using copies of page 29, teach your students how to determine the estimated time of arrival with this formula:

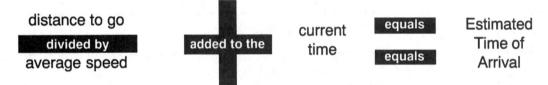

After your students demonstrate their understanding of how to estimate arrival times, you can use page 30 to have them determine both arrival times and departure times, based on places they would really like to go to.

As part of these activities, explain to your students that some countries and the military use a 24-hour system to describe times, while some other countries, including the U.S.A., use an A. M. / P. M. system.

A.M./P.M. System	24 hour System	A.M./P.M. System	24 hour System
1:00 A.M. =	1:00 hours	1:00 P.M. =	13:00 hours
2:00 A.M =	2:00 hours	2:00 P.M. =	14:00 hours
3:00 A.M. =	3:00 hours	3:00 P.M. =	15:00 hours
4:00 A.M. =	4:00 hours	4:00 P.M. =	16:00 hours
5:00 A.M. =	5:00 hours	5:00 P.M. =	17:00 hours
6:00 A.M. =	6:00 hours	6:00 P.M. =	18:00 hours
7:00 A.M. =	7:00 hours	7:00 P.M. =	19:00 hours
8:00 A.M. =	8:00 hours	8:00 P.M. =	20:00 hours
9:00 A.M. =	9:00 hours	9:00 P.M. =	21:00 hours
10:00 A.M. =	10:00 hours	10:00 P.M. =	22:00 hours
11:00 A.M. =	11:00 hours	11:00 P.M. =	23:00 hours
12:00 Noon =	12:00 hours	12:00 Midnight =	24:00 hours
		14:00 would be stated as "Fourteen hundred hours."	

Estimating Arrival Times
Introductory Activity

When families are on the road, the driver is often asked when you're going to get to the next stop. Passengers can figure out the answer the same way the driver does. You don't have to make difficult calculations. This is a good use for estimation.

You need three pieces of information to determine your probable arrival time:

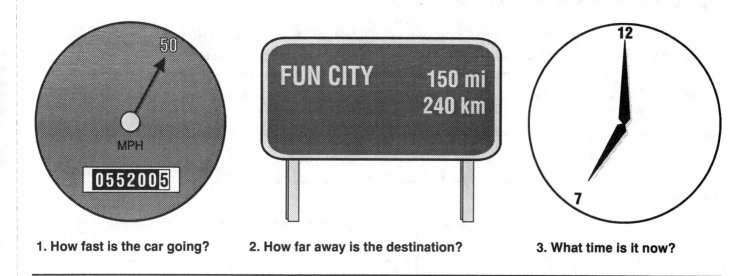

1. How fast is the car going?   **2. How far away is the destination?**   **3. What time is it now?**

On the open road, a car averages around 50 miles per hour or 80 kilometers per hour. If you divide that number into the distance to your destination, it will tell you about how many hours it will take to get there. Adding those hours to the current time gives you your estimated time of arrival.

In the example pictured above, the car is going 50 mi/hr (80 km/hr). The destination is 150 miles (240 km) away. If you divide 150 by 50 you get 3 hours. If you divide 240 by 80, you also get 3 hours. It works the same with either system of measurement. If the current time were 7:00 in the morning, the estimated time of arrival would be 3 hours later: 10:00 o'clock that morning.

Try these examples, using 50 mi/hr (80 km/hr) as your average speed:

Average Speed	Distance to Destination	Current Time	Estimated Time of Arrival
50 mi/hr	350 miles	9:00 a.m.	
80 km/hr	400 kilometers	11:00 hrs.	
50 mi/hr	225 miles	1:00 p.m.	
80 km/hr	280 kilometers	14:00 hrs.	
50 mi/hr	375 miles	9:30 a.m.	

Math on a Trip

Let's Get There on Time
Application Activity

Let's apply what you've learned about estimating travel and arrival time. Select five places you would like to visit that could be reached by car in one day. List the locations on the chart below. Use a roadmap or atlas to determine the distance from your home to these locations and fill in that column of the chart. Using 50 mi/hr (80 km/hr) as the average driving speed, estimate how long it would take to reach each of these locations. Also estimate the arrival times, based on a 9:00 A.M. departure.

Destination	Travel Time	Estimated Time of <u>Arrival</u> with 9:00 A.M. Departure

Now let's look at it another way. Instead of always leaving at 9:00 A.M., suppose it were the arrival time that you wanted to standardize. Select 5 more destinations and estimate the travel time as before. Then, decide upon a departure time that would have you arrive at 6:00 P.M. (18:00 hours).

Destination	Travel Time	<u>Departure</u> time so you arrive at 6:00 P.M. (18:00)

Math Games for the Road

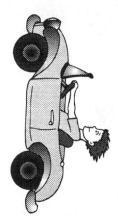

Sometimes when you are on a family trip, there will be a quiet stretch without much to look at. Here are some games you can learn and practice at school and later teach the family on the road.

Fizz

Players rotate turns counting up from one. Any time a number comes up that has a five in it or that is a multiple of five, the player says, "fizz." Learning the game using fives makes it easy to get started. Each time a mistake is made, the player drops out. The last player left is the winner. If or when "fizz" is too easy, move on to "buzz" and beyond. Here is what "fizz" would sound like:

1... 2... 3... 4... fizz... 6... 7... 8... 9... fizz... 11... 12... 13... 14... fizz... 16... 17... 18... 19... fizz... 21...

Buzz

Play just like "fizz," only say "buzz" for numbers that have a seven in them or are multiples of seven. You can see that it is a little harder using sevens because the numbers with sevens in them aren't always the same as the numbers that are multiples of seven.

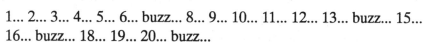

1... 2... 3... 4... 5... 6... buzz... 8... 9... 10... 11... 12... 13... buzz... 15... 16... buzz... 18... 19... 20... buzz...

Fizz-Buzz

If you are good at playing "buzz," you are ready to try "Fizz-Buzz." Just put the two tasks together.

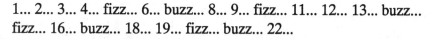

1... 2... 3... 4... fizz... 6... buzz... 8... 9... fizz... 11... 12... 13... buzz... fizz... 16... buzz... 18... 19... fizz... buzz... 22...

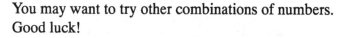

You may want to try other combinations of numbers.
Good luck!

Determining Fuel Efficiency
Teacher Instructions

Teach your students the term "fuel efficiency," or as it is called in America, "gas mileage." Describe the significance of fuel efficiency as it relates to the cost of taking a trip.

Explain that fuel efficiency tells how far a car will go with one gallon or one liter of fuel. More efficient cars go farther than less efficient cars do with the same amount of fuel. Fuel efficiency varies according to the driving conditions. A car won't go as far on an uphill road as on a flat one. A car won't go as far in the city as it will on the open road.

Show your students how to figure out the fuel efficiency of a car:

1. Fill the fuel tank.

2. Write down the number on the odometer.

3. Drive until you need more fuel.

4. Fill the fuel tank.

5. Write down how many gallons or liters were used.

6. Write down the number on the odometer.

7. Subtract the new odometer number from the old.

8. Divide the answer by the gallons or liters used.

page 33

page 34

In order to average out the differences in fuel efficiency when driving under a variety of conditions, this procedure would be repeated serveral times, and the results would be averaged.

If you divide gallons into miles, the fuel efficiency will be in "miles per gallon." If you divide liters into kilometers, the fuel efficiency will be in "kilometers per liter."

Use copies of page 33 to have your students practice the calculation of fuel efficiency. Then, they will be able to use copies of page 34 to calculate the fuel efficiency of their family car at home.

Math on a Trip

Compare These Cars
Introductory Activity

Car advertisements often talk about the "fuel efficiency" of the cars they sell. In the U.S.A., fuel efficiency is also referred to as "gas mileage." What does fuel efficiency mean?

Fuel efficiency tells how far a car will go with just one gallon or liter of fuel. Not all cars are the same. Some go farther than others with the same amount of fuel.

Compare the cars below. Subtract the first odometer reading from the second to see how far the car went. Divide that number by the amount of fuel used to go that far. The answer will be the fuel efficiency.

Car	Odometer Readings (mi or km) 1st Reading	2nd Reading	Fuel Used (gallons or liters)	Fuel Efficiency (mi/gal or km/l)
Red Car	55200	55600	15.0	
Blue Car	34350	34800	12.5	
Green Car	86952	87347	13.2	

Which car above had the best fuel efficiency?

Which car above had the worst fuel efficiency?

How fuel efficient is your family car?

Application Activity

Now that you know how to calculate fuel efficiency, you can check on the efficiency of your own family car. Rather than doing just one calculation, do several and average the answers for a more accurate result. This is particularly important if the car is used in a variety of ways. Efficiency will be much higher on the open road than in the city.

Here is a chart you can use to record several efficiency checks:

Trial Number	1st Odometer Reading	2nd Odometer Reading	Distance Traveled	Fuel Used	Fuel Efficiency
1					
2					
3					
4					
5					
6					
7					
8					
9					
10					

Circle which units of measurement you used for your calculations:

$$\frac{miles}{gallon} \qquad\qquad \frac{kilometers}{liter}$$

Average Fuel Efficiency

Math on a Trip

Checking the Check

Use these on separate occasions for a quick math activity. Tell your students that there is a mistake on the check. Ask them to write the correction on the check to show how much they owe or are owed.

Snack Bar Receipt

5 Sandwiches @ .50	$3.00
6 Drinks @ .25	2.00
subtotal	5.00
10% tip	.50
Total	$5.50

Good Eats!

Theater Receipt

2 ADULT TICKETS @ $7.75	$11.50
2 CHILD TICKETS @ $3.75	5.50
	17.00
TAX 5%	.85
TOTAL	17.85

Thanks for coming!

Motel Receipt

ROOM RATE	$	59.
NO. OF NIGHTS	X	3
TOTAL		177.00
DISCOUNT	10%	17.70
TOTAL	$	194.70

come again!

Market Receipt

Groceries	$27.98
.25 coupon	
.50 coupon	
.10 coupon	
Total	$26.04

Thanks!

Adding It All Up
Teacher Instructions

Wow! We are spending a lot!

Adding up the total costs for a vacation trip can be a real eye-opener for youngsters. After doing activities like these, teachers often get thank-you notes from their students' parents. All of a sudden, their children are more appreciative of what it takes to provide a nice vacation.

Another value of these activities is to show a purpose for using estimations. To get the impact of a vacation's cost, you don't have to know the exact figures. With only approximations, you can still get that "Oh my gosh!" feeling as the total adds up.

Before doing these activities, students will tend to think only of ticket prices, without noticing the "overhead" that it takes to cover all of the related expenses. The "adding it all up" activities put all of the expenditures on the table in full view.

Page 37 provides approximate costs for six components of a family vacation. Students will calculate the totals in each category and then sum up all six. This is a classroom activity based on an imaginary trip.

Page 38 is for planning an actual family trip. This could either be a trip the student wishes the family would take or one that the family is actually planning. Although the idea is for the student to use real costs, they can still be approximate.

Putting It All Together
Introductory Activity

The activities in this book have focused on travel-related expenses one at a time. Now let's consider the total of all of these expenditures. Add up the charges below to calculate the approximate cost of this family vacation.

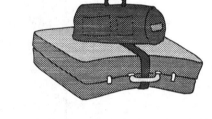

Rental Car
Per day $22.00
six days   x   6

Hotel
Per night $89.00
six days   x   6

Amusement Park
3-day *Adult* $27.00
two adults   x   2

3-day *Child* $18.00
two children   x   2

Family total =

Meals
Per day $120.00
six days   x   6

Other Activities
Per day $40.00
three days   x   3

Round Trip Flight
Per ticket $85.00
for family   x   4

Total cost for this trip:

It is important to estimate the expenses for a trip *before* making specific plans and buying tickets. Sometimes we tend to pay attention only to the major expenses in advance, and find later that we ended up spending twice as much as we had expected.

Note: Use this page to estimate the cost of trips you would really like to make or that your family is actually planning to take. Use approximate numbers.

Budget for a Trip
Application Activity

Expense	Subtotals
Public Transportation - getting there or while there	_____
Driving the Family Car: cost per day driving days _____ X _____ =	_____
Lodging: per night total nights _____ X _____ =	_____
Meals: total meals number of people meal cost per person _____ X _____ X _____ =	_____
Activities: per day total days _____ X _____ =	_____
Other Expenses: (describe below) _____ =	_____
TOTAL COST	

Foreign Travel
Teacher Instructions

Everyday-math gets even more interesting when you travel to other countries. Travelers going to and coming from the U.S.A. run into problems because the U.S. uses measurement systems that are different from most of the other countries of the world. The activities on the following pages deal with some of those differences. Calculators will come in handy here.

Measurement	Units of measurement in the U.S.	Units in most of the rest of the world
Time	afternoon switches from A.M. to P.M.	24-hour clock - no A.M. and P.M.
Money	dollars and cents	each country is different
Weight	pounds and ounces	kilograms and grams
Liquid volume	quarts and ounces	liters and milliliters
Distance	miles	kilometers
Length	yards and inches	meters and centimeters
Temperature	Fahrenheit degrees	Celsius degrees

When traveling in foreign countries, you don't have to keep converting back and forth between the systems. Instead, you try to get used to the system where you are. To do this, you have to get a "feel" for what a unit of measurement represents. If you say to a student, "show me with your fingers what a centimeter is," and the student can come pretty close, that's what you're after.

It is more important to have the concept clear than to be able to calculate the answer to the second decimal point. If you don't work on developing these concepts, you may find that your students can learn to get the calculations right, but not have a clue what the numbers represent.

In addition to working with the calculations involved in these activities, ask your students questions like these:

Ask an American student:
- What does it feel like at 40ºC?
- About how many liters of fuel would fill the tank?
- About how much do you weigh in kilograms?
- About how many kilometers to the market?

Ask a European Student:
- What does it feel like at 40ºF?
- How many gallons of fuel would fill the tank?
- About how much do you weigh in pounds?
- About how many miles to the market?

 Math on a Trip

Time Flies
Introductory Activity

When the sun is straight up, we call it "noon," but it can't be noon all around the world at the same time. That's why we divide the Earth into 24 time zones. Each zone is one hour different from the next. As you travel east, the time is one hour later as you go from zone to zone. It gets one hour earlier as you travel west to a different zone.

Here is a map of an imaginary country with **four time zones**, each 1 hour different, later to the east.

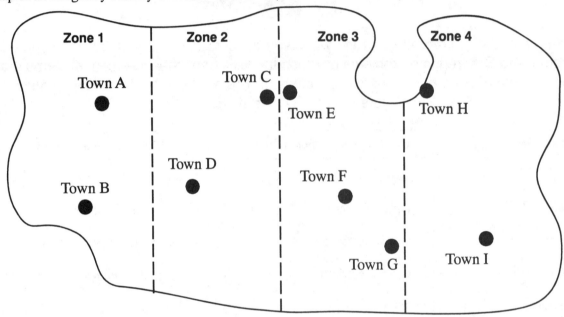

See if you can figure out what time it is in the locations below and fill in the blanks.

If it is this time below in the named location...what time would it be in this other place?			
location	time	location	time
Town A	8:00 A.M.	Town F	_____
Town C	12:00 Noon	Town E	_____
Town I	10:00 P.M. (22:00)	Town D	_____
Town B	3:00 A.M.	Town H	_____
Town E	7:00 P.M. (19:00)	Town G	_____
Town H	12:00 Midnight (24:00)	Town B	_____
Town C	11:00 A.M.	Town A	_____
Town G	6:00 A.M.	Town E	_____

Arrival Times
Application Activity

Earlier we estimated arrival times when traveling by car. When you take a long trip by air, the arrival time is affected because you will be crossing time zones.

The chart below shows departure locations and times, flight durations, and destinations. By adding the flight duration to the departure time, you get the arrival time as it would appear on a clock in the airport you left. To know what time it will say on the clock in the airport where you land, you have to take time zones into account.

Use an atlas to find out how many time zone lines the flight will cross to determine the arrival time on the clock in the destination airport. For each zone line crossed while travelling east, add one hour to the arrival time. For each zone line crossed while traveling west, subtract one hour from the arrival time.

Departure Place	Departure Time	Flight Duration	Destination	Zone Lines Crossed	Arrival Time
Seattle, Washington	9:00 a.m.	2 hours	Denver, Colorado		
Miami, Florida	3:00 p.m. (15:00)	3 hours	Billings, Montana		
Atlanta, Georgia	11:00 a.m.	2 hours	Boston, Mass.		
New York City, N.Y.	5:00 p.m. (17:00)	5 hours	Los Angeles, Calif.		
San Francisco, Cal.	Noon	9 hours	London, England		

Don't forget to call home

Once you have arrived at your destination, you may want to call family and friends. The problem is that the time that is convenient for you to call may not be a convenient time for them to hear from you. Suppose you were in the locations at the times listed on the left side of the chart below. If you made a call to the locations on the right, what time would it be when the phone rings there?

Your Location	Time where you are	Location of the relative	Time where the relative is
Rome, Italy	10:00 P.M. (22:00)	Washington, D.C.	
Tokyo, Japan	9:00 A.M.	Portland, Oregon	
Honolulu, Hawaii	8:00 P.M. (20:00)	Kansas City, Kansas	
Bogota, Colombia	1:00 P.M. (13:00)	Philadelphia, Penn.	
Anchorage, Alaska	7:00 P.M. (19:00)	Phoenix, Arizona	

Math on a Trip

Money Exchange Rates

England	France	Germany	Italy
$ x .7 = Pounds	$ x 5.6 = Francs	$ x 1.7 = Deutch Marks	$ x 1500 = Lira
Mexico	**Australia**	**Russia**	**South Africa**
$ x 3.3 = Pesos	$ x 1.4 = Australian Dollars	$ x 2000 = Rubles	$ x 3.5 = Rands
Spain	**Switzerland**	**Austria**	**Canada**
$ x 135 = Pesetas	$ x 1.4 = Swiss Francs	$ x 11.6 = Shillings	$ x 1.3 = Canadian Dollars

When you go to a foreign country, you have to change your kind of money into their kind so you can pay for the things you do or buy there. Even in countries that use the same name for their money that your country does, the value can be different.

The exchange rate changes just about every day. To know how much you would get for one U.S. dollar on a particular day, you would look at a chart like the one above.

On the above day, how much would you get for:	
$100 in England: _____ Pounds	$150 in Russia: _____ Rubles
$50 in France: _____ Francs	$25 in South Africa: _____ Rands
$75 in Germany: _____ Deutchmarks	$130 in Spain: _____ Pesetas
$110 in Italy: _____ Lira	$60 in Switzerland: ____ Swiss Francs
$200 in Mexico: _____ Pesos	$275 in Austria: _____ Shillings
$80 in Australia: ____ Australian Dollars	$45 in Canada: _____ Canadian Dollars

Weights are Different When You Travel

When you go to the market in a foreign country, it is hard to tell how much to buy because the units of measurement for weights are different. See if you can fill in the blanks below to show the equivalent weights.

U.S. Markets
pounds x 0.45
gives you kilograms

European Markets
kilograms x 2.2
gives you pounds

U.S.		European
3 lbs	=	kg
lbs	=	3 kg
12 lbs	=	kg
lbs	=	15 kg
40 lbs	=	kg

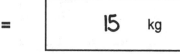

U.S. Markets
ounces x 28
gives you grams

European Markets
grams x 0.035
gives you ounces

U.S.		European
8 oz	=	g
oz	=	300 g
15 oz	=	g
oz	=	450 g
32 oz	=	g

Math on a Trip

Volumes are Different When You Travel

When you go to the market in a foreign country, it is hard to tell how much to buy because the units of measurement for volumes are different. See if you can fill in the blanks below to show the equivalent volumes.

U.S. Stores
quarts x .95
gives you liters

Asian Stores
litersx 1.06
gives you quarts

2 qt	=	l
qt	=	7 l
5 qt	=	l
qt	=	2 l
3 qt	=	l

U.S. Stores
ounces x 29.6
gives you milliliters

Asian Stores
milliliters x 0.03
gives you ounces

4 oz	=	ml
oz	=	175 ml
20 oz	=	ml
oz	=	350 ml
12 oz	=	ml

Math on a Trip

Lengths are Different When You Travel

When you go to the market in a foreign country, it is hard to tell how long things are or how far away places are because the units of measurement for lengths and distances are different. See if you can fill in the blanks below to show the equivalent lengths and distances.

In the United States
inches x 2.54
gives you centimeters

In South America
centimeters x .04
gives you inches

2 in	=	cm
in	=	12 cm
7 in	=	cm

In the United States
yards x 0.9
gives you meters

In South America
meters x 1.1
gives you yards

4 yd	=	m
yd	=	5 m
9 yd	=	m

In the United States
miles x 1.6
gives you kilometers

In South America
kilometers x 0.6
gives you miles

25 mi	=	km
mi	=	21 km
43 mi	=	km

   Math on a Trip

Temperatures are Different When You Travel

When you go to a foreign country, it is hard to tell how hot it is because the units of measurement for temperature are different. See if you can fill in the blanks below to show the equivalent temperatures.

In the United States
°F - 32 x 5/9
gives you °C

In Africa
°C x 9/5 +32
gives you °F

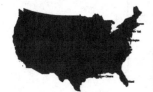

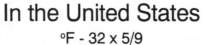

In the United States		In Africa
41°F	=	°C
°F	=	10°C
59°F	=	°C
°F	=	25°C
98.6°F	=	°C
°F	=	60°C
86°F	=	°C
°F	=	35°C

Math on a Trip

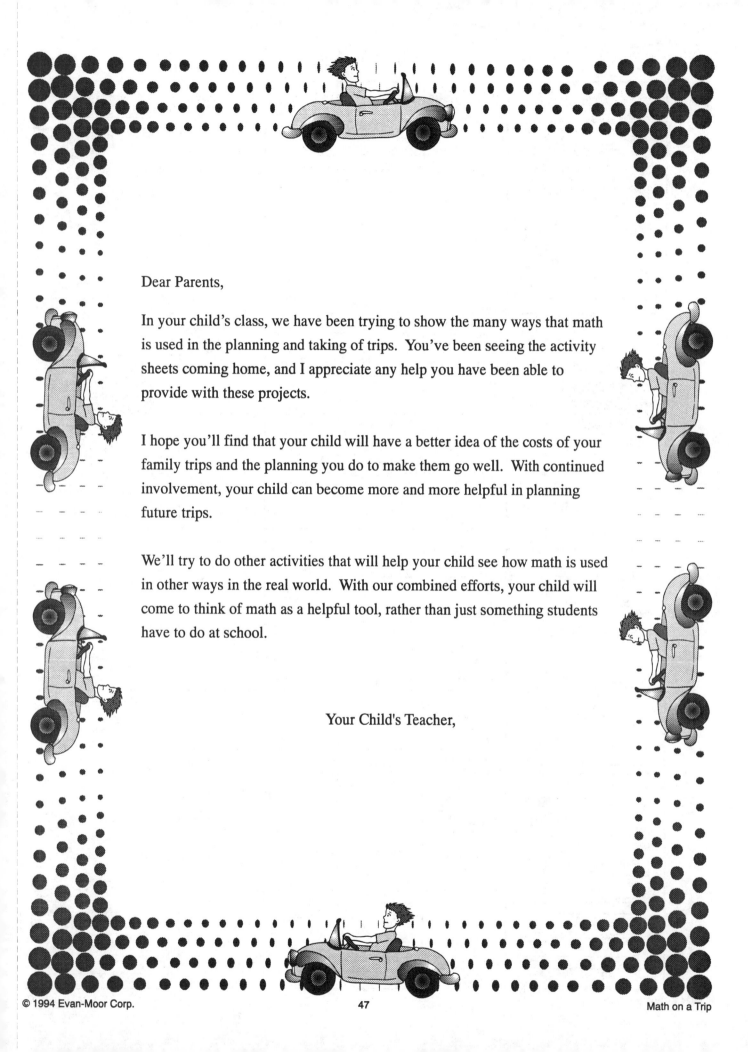

Dear Parents,

In your child's class, we have been trying to show the many ways that math is used in the planning and taking of trips. You've been seeing the activity sheets coming home, and I appreciate any help you have been able to provide with these projects.

I hope you'll find that your child will have a better idea of the costs of your family trips and the planning you do to make them go well. With continued involvement, your child can become more and more helpful in planning future trips.

We'll try to do other activities that will help your child see how math is used in other ways in the real world. With our combined efforts, your child will come to think of math as a helpful tool, rather than just something students have to do at school.

Your Child's Teacher,

Answer Key

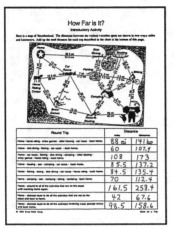

page 5 — How Far is It? (Introductory Activity)

Round Trip	Distance	
	miles	kilometers
Home - horse riding - arrow games - roller blowing - car races - back home.	88 mi	141 km
Home - diet diving - fishing - car races - back home.	60	107.4
Home - car races - fishing - skin diving - camping - roller blading - arrow games - horse riding - back home.	108	173
Home - boating - zoo - camping - car races - back home.	85.5	137.2
Home - fishing - boating - skin diving - car races - horse riding - back home.	84.5	135.4
Home - camping - zoo - camping - biking - camping - back home.	70	112.4
Home - around to all the activities that are on the onset until reaching home again.	161.5	258.4
Home - shortest route to do all the activities that are not on the onset and back to home.	42	67.6
Home - shortest route to do all the activities involving most (except arrow) and back home.	98.5	158.6

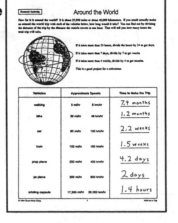

page 7 — Around the World (Related Activity)

Vehicles	Approximate Speeds		Time to Make the Trip
walking	5 m/hr	8 km/hr	7.4 months
bike	30 m/hr	48 km/hr	1.2 months
car	65 m/hr	100 km/hr	2.2 weeks
train	100 m/hr	160 km/hr	1.5 weeks
prop plane	250 m/hr	400 km/hr	4.2 days
jet plane	500 m/hr	800 km/hr	2 days
orbiting capsule	17,500 m/hr	28,000 km/hr	1.4 hours

page 9 — Look at All the Choices!

Activity	Total Price for this Family	Discount Price for this Family
Theme Park	40.00	36.00
The Big Game	76.50	68.85
Water Playland	30.00	27.00
Family Theater	21.20	19.08
Zooquarium	34.92	31.43
Advanturama	48.64	43.78

page 11

Anwers will vary depending on parents' estimates of prices.

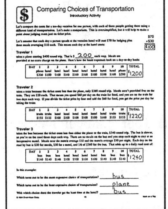

page 15 — Comparing Choices of Transportation (Introductory Activity)

Traveler 1 ... 200 each way ... TOTAL 1200

Traveler 2 ... TOTAL 1220

Traveler 3 ... TOTAL 1240

Which turns out to be the most expensive choice of transportation? **bus**

Which turns out to be the least expensive choice of transportation? **plane**

With which choice does the traveler get the least time at the hotel? **bus**

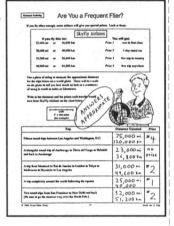

page 17 — Are You a Frequent Flier? (Related Activity)

ANSWERS ARE APPROXIMATE

Trip	Distance Traveled	Prize
Fifteen round trips between Los Angeles and Washington, D.C.	75,000 mi / 120,000 km	#4
A triangular round trip of Anchorage to Tierra del Fuego to Helsinki and back to Anchorage	23,000 mi / 36,800 km	no prize
A trip from Montreal to Rio de Janeiro to London to Tokyo to Melbourne to Honolulu to Los Angeles	31,000 mi / 49,600 km	#2
A trip supposedly around the world following the equator	25,000 mi / 40,000	#1
Two round trips from San Francisco to New Delhi and back (the men to go the shortest way, over the North Pole.)	32,000 mi / 51,200 km	#2

page 18 — Let's Rent a Car

You want a car for three days in a U.S. city; Friday, Saturday, and Sunday. You plan to drive the car less than 600 miles.

Company	Total Cost
1. Rattling Rents	$120
2. Vroom Rentals	$125
3. Awesome Autos	$130
4. Comfy Cars	$135

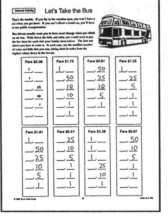

page 19 — Let's Take the Bus (Related Activity)

Fare $2.36	Fare $1.72	Fare $0.81	Fare $1.33
1	1	50	1
1	50	25	25
25	10	10	5
10	10	1	1
1	1	1	1

Fare $1.91	Fare $0.45	Fare $3.36	Fare $0.87
1	25	1	50
50	10	1	10
25	5	1	10
10	5	25	1
5		10	1
1		1	

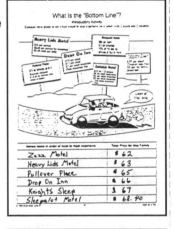

page 21 — What Is the "Bottom Line"? (Introductory Activity)

	Total Price for this Family
Zzzz Motel	$62
Heavy Lids Motel	$63
Pullover Place	$65
Drop On Inn	$66
Knights Sleep	$67
Sleepalot Motel	$68.40

page 23 — How About a trailer? Should we rent or buy? (Related Activity)

If a trailer rents for $50 per day, how much would it cost your family for a two-week (14- day) vacation? **$700**

If the trailer costs $15,000... How much would the trailer cost altogether? **$19,200**

How many months are there in one year? **12**

How many months are there in four years? **48**

What would your monthly payments be if you were to pay off the total cost for the new trailer over the four-year period? **$400/mo**

The only way that buying the trailer would be a good idea for financial reasons involved... **96 days/year**

About how many months is that? **about 3 months**

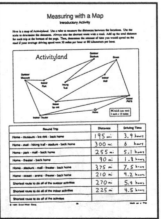

page 25 — Measuring with a Map (Introductory Activity)

Round Trip	Distance	Driving Time
Home - museum - ice rink - back home	195 mi	3.9 hours
Home - maul - hiking trail - stadium - back home	300 mi	6 hours
Home - park - mall - back home	255 mi	5.1 hours
Home - theater - back home	90 mi	1.8 hours
Home - stadium - mall - theater - back home	375 mi	7.5 hours
Home - ocean - arena - theater - back home	210 mi	4.2 hours
Shortest route to do all the outdoor activities	270 mi	5.4 hours
Shortest route to do all the indoor activities	225 mi	4.5 hours
Shortest route to do all the activities		

page 27 — Lost your Luggage? (Related Activity)

Insurance Form			
	number lost	allowance per item	Total allowance per category
shirts	7	12.00	84.00
blouses	5	14.00	70.00
sweaters	3	13.00	39.00
shoes	4	27.00	100.00
jeans	6	18.00	108.00
skirts	5	15.00	75.00
dresses	4	20.00	80.00
underwear	15	5.00	75.00
shoes (pair)	4	20.00	80.00
stockings (pairs)	16	3.00	48.00
belts	2	9.00	18.00
ties	3	6.00	18.00
		Subtotal	745.00
The company does not pay for the first $200 of the loss. This is referred to as a "deductible."		Deductible	-200.00
		Grand Total	515.00